Exploring tough questions facing youth today

KEEPING THE GARDEN

A Faith Response to God's Creation

The Pastoral Center

ISBN 978-1-949628-15-9
Printed in the United States of America.
10 9 8 7 6 5 4 3 2 1   22 21 20 19

Published by The Pastoral Center, http://pastoral.center.

Developed in partnership with MennoMedia and Brethren Press. Series editors: Fumiaki Tosu, Ann Naffziger, and Paul Canavese. *Keeping the Garden:* Writers, Tim and Donita Wiebe-Neufeld. Project editor, Lani Wright. Staff editors, Susan E. Janzen, Julie Garber, and James Deaton. Updated design, Paul Stocksdale.

All rights reserved. Purchase of this book includes a license to reproduce this resource for use in a single parish, school, or other similar organization. You are allowed to share and make unlimited copies only for use within the organization that licensed it. If you serve more than one organization, each should purchase its own license. You may not post this document to any web site without explicit permission to do so. Outside of these conditions, no part of this book may be reproduced in any form or by any means, electronic or mechanical, including photocopying, recording, taping, or via any retrieval system, without the written permission of The Pastoral Center, 1212 Versailles Ave., Alameda, CA 94501. Thank you for cooperating with our honor system regarding our licenses.

For questions or to order additional copies or licenses, please call 1-844-727-8672 or visit http://pastoral.center.

Portions of this work © 2019 by The Pastoral Center / PastoralCenter.com. Adapted and published with permission from Generation Why Bible Studies. © 1996, 2014 Brethren Press, Elgin, IL 60120 and MennoMedia, Harrisonburg, VA 22803, U.S.A. All rights reserved.

Unless otherwise noted, the Scripture passages contained herein are from the *New Revised Standard Version of the Bible*, copyright © 1989 by the National Council of the Churches of Christ in the United States of America. Used by permission. All rights reserved.

Bible-based Explorations of Issues Facing Youth

» OVERVIEW

When conversing online, the acronym IRL stands for "in real life." The virtual world of social media, text chats, blogs, and more have the power to remove us from the real world. What we experience online can skew our perspective on what it means to be human. It can numb us, incite us, distract us, depress us, confuse us, and make us rude or impatient. Strangely, this supposedly "social" and "connected" technology can profoundly disconnect us from others.

Religious faith can also place us in a bubble, especially when it distances us from others. When we keep the prophetic message at a safe distance, obscured in theological language and abstractions, we are missing the whole point. And when we see our parish as an insider club that serves itself, we can forget the radically inclusive message entrusted to us: God's love is for *everyone*, and God expects us to transform the *whole world* through that love.

Through the incarnation, God showed up in the real world to show us that our faith is not just about talking the talk, but also walking the walk. It can be risky. It can be confusing. It can hurt. But living out our faith can also bring us great purpose, peace, and joy.

This series connects the Bible with the tough questions that youth (and adults) encounter in their neighborhood, in school, among friends, and even online. This process will help you as a leader break open these issues in a fun and meaningful way, sparking conversation and the kind of life change Jesus invites us to embrace.

» THE ROLE OF PARENTS

As children enter middle school and high school, they become more independent, self-reliant, and, well, self-centered. This can bring parents to make assumptions that this is the time to step back, giving their child more space to form their identity. While there is truth to that at some level (adolescents definitely shouldn't be smothered), this is a stage of life when parents should in fact *lean in*. The apparent confidence and bluster youth show on the outside can mask the insecurity and confusion on the inside. Youth need their parents to be involved more than ever.

» WHOLE FAMILY FORMATION

Parents are the primary teachers of their own children, and parishes are waking up to the fact that faith formation programs need to bring parents into the process if they hope to see faith passed on to the next generation. Recent studies give us more and more evidence that the role of parents is the most important factor in determining whether a child will embrace faith as they move toward adulthood. Research from the Center for the Applied Research on the Apostolate shows that parents who talk about their faith and show through their actions that their faith is important to them are more likely to have children who remain Catholic.

More about Whole Family Formation

To learn more about how your parish can take a comprehensive whole family approach to faith formation, visit **GrowingUpCatholic.com**.

While whole family events with elementary-aged children are on the rise, the role of parents can be an afterthought in youth ministry. We have designed the sessions in this series to work with or without parents present, and we encourage you to offer them as parent-child events.

If you choose to involve parents, it is important to consider before each session how to best do so. Many of the activities in this series are high-energy, creative, or silly. Some parents may need some encouragement to get out of their heads and have fun with the group. A few activities involving physical contact would be inappropriate for parents and youth to participate together, and we have noted them as such.

There are a number of ways to approach discussions with parent participation. Unless you have a small group, you will likely want to break into smaller groups for conversation. Some youth may be self-conscious and unable to be completely honest and open in a group situation with a parent present. For this reason, you may choose in some cases to assign parents to different groups from their own children, or to have separate parent and child groups altogether. Be sure to cover expectations around confidentiality. It is inappropriate for a parent (or youth) to share with another parent what their child said in a small group.

Note that even if parents and their children do not share all conversations together in the session, they will still have a valuable shared experience and can have extended conversations about it later.

THANK YOU

The role you play in gathering, animating, praying with, and forming youth is a valuable one. Thank you for all you do to serve the church and its families!

Bible-based Explorations of Issues Facing Youth

KEEPING THE GARDEN
A Faith Response to God's Creation

>> INTRODUCTION

Most of us are aware our environment is facing serious problems. We hear staggering stories in the media—global warming, climate change, species extinction, pollution—the list seems unending. Yet, how often do we think of these as *faith issues*, or a crisis of theology? What role could faith communities be taking to call us to more just, relational, and sustainable ways of honoring God's creation?

On Pentecost 2015, Pope Francis published a papal encyclical letter, *On Care for Our Common Home* (*Laudato Si'*) to address these issues from a Catholic perspective. The letter, addressed to all people—not just to Catholics or Christians—looks at the reality of the ecological crisis, its causes, and possible solutions. Pope Francis' teaching is rooted in the Gospels, as well as previous papal documents and the teaching of bishops' conferences from around the globe.

The heart of Pope Francis' teaching in the encyclical is his affirmation that the environmental crisis is not only about polluted land, water, and air, but also about dangerous attitudes towards other human beings, as well as economic practices that harm people and the environment. He advocates an "integral ecology" that encompasses concern for the environment, the protection of all human life, concrete acts of solidarity with the poor, and ethical conduct in economic affairs.

This unit helps participants examine what the Bible has to say about these same issues. Specifically, we will explore whether the ancient book of Genesis can shed light on today's environmental challenges.

Genesis clearly answers with an emphatic yes! Genesis comes at the beginning of the Bible not just because it tells of the beginning of things but because it establishes all the grounding for faith, including who God is, and how we humans are supposed to relate to creation and to God. Genesis is not a scientific description of the world that explains everything rationally, nor a mythological description that previews a reality we will enjoy in another realm. The earth is God's, and creation is a "book" like Genesis that reveals Life and light at the heart of all that has life. That is why we must take care of it. We do not need any reason other than that God is embedded in this treasure that we are to hold and protect. If we believe God made the world, our relationship with God's good gift of creation means ensuring that it continues to function according to God's design.

Preparation Alert >>>>

In each session is printed a "Unit Affirmation," which may be used as a thread connecting all the sessions. Before the first session, make a poster with the words of the affirmation, so that all may learn it together. This affirmation is also printed on one of the handout sheets available for this session.

>>> EXTENDER SESSION

Extender sessions suggest special activities related to the issue of the unit. They help accommodate the diversity of parish schedules. Since each unit is undated, participants may study units in their entirety and still participate in special events of the parish that get scheduled simultaneously with youth group time. Extender sessions can be used anytime, but the one for this unit best follows **Session 4**. Calculate now whether or not you will be using the extender session.

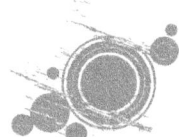

By affirming God as creator, we affirm that creation should function according to God's intention for it. Genesis gives us some handles with which to discern those intentions for creation. Right from "the beginning," the Bible is a meditation on the mystery of creation, the role of darkness and the interplay of light at its core.

First, creation is good. This assessment is not reserved just for humanity. Each step of creation was affirmed by the Creator. It was only when the whole of creation was complete that God pronounced the entire world as "very good." (*On Care for Our Common Home*, 65)

Second, God created the world to be full of life, making every kind of plant and wildlife, blessing all. God has created remarkably diverse plants, animals, and people, and delights in the variety. (*On Care for Our Common Home*, 69, 86)

Third, God has woven humanity into creation with special responsibility. Our ability to name creation suggests a caring, integral relationship with our world. Creation provides for our needs; in return we are to till it and keep it. We are to ensure that the earth continues to bring forth life and provides for human need for generations to come. (*On Care for Our Common Home*, 67-68)

To care humbly and properly for the earth, we are to respect the limits under which we have been created. Our covenant with the Creator establishes limits on human behavior, but when our wills exceed the limits, we degrade our relationship with others, our relationship with creation, and our relationship with God. We must recognize gaps between our needs and wants. We are to look beyond ourselves to see how our use of resources affects people in other areas of the world, threatens the future of creation, and separates us from God. (*On Care for Our Common Home*, 66, 238-240)

Finally, we are to live into the message of hope. By responding faithfully to God, we can repair our relationship with creation. Many problems in our environment are the result of many people doing little things. Entering into a sacred relationship with God's creation will mean many people making little changes to their lives. (*On Care for Our Common Home*, 205, 222-227)

THE TEACHING PLAN: The parts of the session guide

> **Faith story.** The session is rooted in this Bible passage.

> **Faith focus.** This is the story of the passage in a nutshell.

> **Session goal.** The entire session is built around this goal. What changes—in knowledge, attitude, and/or action—do you desire in your group?

> **Materials needed and advance preparation.** This is what you will need if the session is to go smoothly. You'll feel more at ease if you've taken care of these details before you meet your group.

>> FROM LIFE TO BIBLE TO LIFE

The teaching plan we use is called *life-centered*. However, when we write each session, we always begin with Scripture. We ask, what does this particular passage say, especially to youth? Each session moves from life to Bible to life. So the Bible is really at the center of this way of teaching.

In every session we try to hit upon a tough question that participants might ask. Find out what questions on this issue are important for your group. Feel free to bring your own input and invite your group members to add their own experiences.

>> TEACHING THE SESSION

The five step-by-step movements will carry you from *life to the Bible and back to life*. Each session takes about 45 to 50 minutes. If there is a handout sheet for the session, take note of any complementary activities and stories.

1. **Focus.** This activity is intended to create a friendly climate within the group and to draw attention to the issue.
2. **Connect.** Talking, drawing, role playing, and other activities invite participants to express their own life experience about the issue. Also use memory, reason, or imagination to get the group thinking about *why* they view the issue the way they do.
3. **Explore the Bible.** With a minimum of lecturing, dig into the faith story and search for answers to questions raised in the first activities. The Insights from Scripture section will help clarify the faith story. Help participants discover how the faith community understands the Bible passage.
4. **Apply** the faith story. This is the "aha!" moment when participants realize the faith story has wisdom for *their* lives.
5. **Respond.** What will the group do about the issue in light of what they have learned from their own experiences set alongside the faith story? How can we live the faith story rather than pass it off as a mere intellectual exercise?

"God's Spirit is felt brooding with boundless eternal love over all, making every lifecell rejoice."

John Muir, 1838–1914

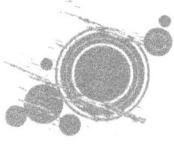

>> LOOK AHEAD

Here are reminders for what you need to do for the next session or two.

>> INSIGHTS FROM SCRIPTURE

Here is a resource for Explore the Bible. Don't try to use all the material given. Take what you need to lead the session and answer questions your group may have. Let the Insights section inspire you to think and study more about the passage for the session.

>> HANDOUT SHEETS

Occasionally, there will be a handout sheet to complement your session. If you choose to use this, make enough copies for the group in advance of the session. These sheets may include questions, stories, agree/disagree exercises, charts, pictures, and other materials to stimulate thinking and discussion.

Generally, no participant preparation is required unless the session plan calls for you to contact selected group members for specific tasks.

Exploring tough questions facing youth today

>>> SESSION 1

A MESS IN GOD'S KITCHEN >>>

>> KEY VERSE

God saw everything that he had made, and indeed, it was very good. (Gen. 1:31a)

>> FAITH STORY

Genesis 1:1-31

>> FAITH FOCUS

The story of creation in Genesis 1 is a primer about who God is and how created beings interconnect. Most importantly, it affirms God as creator of the world and all that is in it. God began with chaos and, in time, invited a life-giving order to take shape. We do not need any reason to hold and protect creation other than that God is embedded in this treasure. If we believe God made the world, our relationship with God's good gift of creation means ensuring that it continues to function according to God's design.

>> SESSION GOAL

Encourage participants to build their care for the environment as a faith response to God the Creator.

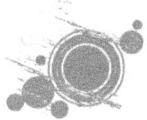

TEACHING PLAN

1. FOCUS 10-12 minutes

Play a game of "Environmental Pictionary" to help participants start thinking about environmental problems. Pictionary is a charade game in which players silently draw pictures to help their team guess the password or phrase.

Divide into two teams. The first team selects one member to be the "drawer." The drawer is given a slip of paper with an environmental concern written on it, and has one minute to draw pictures while the rest of the team tries to guess the environmental topic.

The drawer cannot use letters, numbers, or symbols (e.g., "$" or "&"). The team must guess the topic *exactly*. The drawer can depict one word at a time, but the team must say the right words together. If time expires, reveal the topic.

>> Materials needed and advance preparation

- Review instructions for "Environmental Pictionary," get a timer, and write topics on small pieces of paper (see Focus).
- Chalkboard/chalk or newsprint/marker
- Make or commission a "dirty kitchen video" (see Connect *Challenge Option*).
- Give copies of "Crammin' about Creation" (on handout sheet) scripts to two people a few days or a week beforehand, and arrange a quick run-through if possible (see Explore the Bible *Option A*).
- Bibles
- Two sets of Legos or wood blocks (Apply *Option C*)
- Paper, pens/pencils
- Contact local parks, a church camp, or environmental agencies for projects for your group (see Respond *Option B*).
- Make a poster with the words of the unit affirmation, or make copies of the handout sheet (see Respond).

In Real Life | Keeping the Garden

> "The Earth, our home, is beginning to look more and more like an immense pile of filth. In many parts of the planet, the elderly lament that once beautiful landscapes are now covered with rubbish."
>
> Pope Francis, *On Care for Our Common Home*, 21.

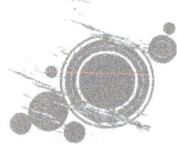

ADDITIONAL RESOURCE

Read Sojourner's blog post, Taking Climate Change Seriously:
http://sojo.net/blogs/2014/06/05/taking-climate-change-seriously

Play then moves to the second team. Alternate turns until everyone has had a chance to draw, or 10 minutes are up.

Possible topics for "Environmental Pictionary":

Extreme weather	Population explosion
Water pollution	Greenhouse effect
Littering	Landfill
Oil spill	Plastics
Smog	Clear-cutting
Extinction	Soil erosion
Rain forest	Radioactive waste
Garbage	Sewage
Recycling	Climate change

2. CONNECT 7 minutes

Ask:

- *Where do you hear about environmental issues?*
- *What is your response to environmental topics when they come up?*
- *Do you think Christians are known for being concerned about the environment?*

Conclude the discussion by saying, *Pope Francis has issued a major teaching on the environment in the form of something called an encyclical. It is basically a long letter addressed to the people of the world, outlining a Christian response to our current crisis. Over the next few weeks, we will read quotes and short excerpts from this letter, in addition to our study of the Bible. The title of this encyclical is* On Care for Our Common Home, *or* Laudato Si'.

Instruct the participants to sit back and close their eyes as you read the following:

Imagine you are hungry. Your stomach is growling loudly enough to be heard clear across the room. School is out and you're going over to a friend's place. The two of you head into the kitchen for a snack. As you walk in, you notice your feet are sticking to the floor; it reminds you of the floor at a movie theatre. Dirty dishes crusted with dried food are piled high on the counters. The garbage in the corner is spilling onto the floor and you can smell something rotten. Your friend tugs a dish out from one of the piles and uses a sleeve to wipe it off before handing it to you. Your friend pushes the cat litter away from in front of the fridge, opens it up, and pulls out a container of leftovers that look suspiciously green. Your friend turns and starts coming towards you....

Ask, *Are you still hungry? Why or why not?*

Extra challenge option: Have one of your group members make a home video of the above scenario, and show it to the group instead of describing it. It could be really fun to make!

Shift to the next activity by saying: *Our world is like a huge kitchen that supplies us with food, water, and air to breathe. And yet, we are leaving it a complete mess. According to the Bible, when we dirty the world, we are dirtying something created by God and that God wants us to care for.*

3. EXPLORE THE BIBLE 10-12 minutes

>>> **Option A:** Present the creation story from Genesis 1 by using the dialogue "Crammin' about Creation" found on the handout sheet for Session 1. Then discuss the questions listed under *Option B*.

>>> **Option B:** Ask participants to consider the following questions as they read Genesis 1:1-31 from the Bible. (Write them where everyone can see them.) Select one person to read the words of God, and alternate other readers in the position of narrator, perhaps switching for each "day" of creation.

Questions for both options:

How long ago does the passage say the world was created?

    (In the beginning! We are not told exactly when.)

Who is said to have created the world?

    (God. The passage assumes this.)

What is at the heart of God's creation?

    (Light. Light of the "first day" is the source of all life.)

Why did God create the world? For what purposes?

- *to fill the earth with life (Gen. 1:12, 20, 22, 25, 28)*
- *to provide for the needs of humanity (Gen. 1:29)*
- *to provide for the needs of all life (Gen. 1:31)*
- *to create something that was very good (Gen. 1:31)*

Finish by saying something like: *We live in a society that is very interested in details. When we think of the beginning of the world, we want to know how things happened, where they took place, and when. The book of Genesis is less concerned with when, where, and how than questions of* **who** *created the world, and* **why**.

4. APPLY 5-8 minutes

The Bible firmly states that all things have been created by God. God took chaos and out of it ordered a creation filled with all sorts of life. God chose to make it a certain way—a way that brings forth life, provides for the needs of all creatures, including humans, and is very good.

>>> **Option A:** When someone invents something or writes something new, they get a trademark, a copyright, or a patent. Using materials you can gather in five minutes or less, create a trademark or copyright for the Creator of the earth. Display (with ID tags) the trademarks somewhere in your church building.

>>> **Option B:** Distribute paper and a pen/pencil to everyone. Allow three minutes to draw something they have made or write something they did that they felt proud of.

When they are finished, exchange the papers with a partner. Have them take 30 seconds or so to explain the writings or drawings. Then instruct *everyone* to tear up the papers they are holding.

Ask: *How did you feel when someone else tore up what you had drawn or written? What happens to the heart of God when we do things that mess up and damage the world?*

All-powerful God,

you are present in the whole universe and in the smallest of your creatures. You embrace with your tenderness all that exists. Pour out upon us the power of your love, that we may protect life and beauty. AMEN

Pope Francis, *On Care for Our Common Home*, 246.

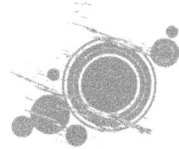

>>> **Option C:** Get into the same teams as for Pictionary. Give each team a set of Legos or wood blocks, and tell them, *You have 4 minutes to build the eighth wonder of the world* (could be a tower, an invention, a sculpture). Have each group briefly explain their creation, then allow each group to gather around the other group's creation to examine it and tinker with it. After a few moments, give groups free reign to wreck the "wonders" they're looking at.

Ask: *How did you feel when someone else wrecked your creation? What happens to the heart of God when we do things that mess up and damage the world?*

UNIT AFFIRMATION

We care for the earth because:

God made it;

God owns it;

God cares for it;

God wills it;

God speaks through it;

God acts in it.

Shantilal Bhagat, in "God's Earth Our Home."

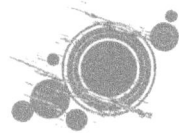

5. RESPOND 8-12 minutes

Help the group identify specific ways they endanger God's creation and ways they help preserve it. Ask these questions:

1. *What specifically threatens the quality of life on our planet?*
2. *How are earth, sky, and sea polluted?*
3. *What motivates humankind to endanger the environment?*
4. *How do young people participate in the destruction of the world God created?*
5. *How do they help preserve it?*

A few things to list if your group needs jumping off points:

Danger:

- wasting natural resources like water, heat, gasoline, electricity, paper
- using (or overusing) products whose manufacture or use contributes to carbon emissions (cars, various plastics)
- littering
- using more of anything than we need
- confusing wants and desires with needs
- being unaware of or ignoring how what we use affects the environment

Preservation:

- Reusing, mending, fixing
- recycling, including composting and mulching
- walking or biking wherever possible
- buying products with little packaging, or providing your own packaging
- planting trees
- buying products made or grown locally

Then choose one of the following options. Whichever option you choose, close in prayer, thanking God for a good creation. Ask for energy, diligence, and ideas for taking care of it. Or use the prayer in the sidebar (page 6), and/or the unit affirmation (included here or on the handout sheet).

>>> **Option A:** "Paying for Poor Choices." Help participants pledge to tax themselves five cents each time in the next week when they make use of an item on the list of dangers generated above. (Make a list for everyone to have with them, and decide on a receptacle for the coins.) *How expensive is it to be careless with God's earth? Is there a higher price you are paying beyond the money?* Send your "tax money" to an environmental protection group like the New Community Project (NewCommunityProject.org) or organizations listed at CatholicCreationCare.com.

>>> **Option B:** Plan a service project to help clean up the environment in your area (e.g., clean up litter, rehabilitate streams in a park, work on reducing soil erosion areas). Decide on dates and times.

INSIGHTS FROM SCRIPTURE

We live in a scientific society, concerned with details and mechanisms. When we think of creation, we want to know exactly when things happened, how long they took, and what methods and recipes God used. The story of creation found in Genesis 1 doesn't answer these questions. It isn't concerned with specific details as much as answering questions of *who*, not when; *why*, not how. It affirms truths about God and creation, and their relationship with each other.

>>> CREATED WITH PURPOSE

Genesis 1 resoundingly affirms God as the creator. God created the earth with purposes in mind, and those purposes were good. The motive for writing the account this way was a concern for cultic order. This account, which could be recited as a litany of worship, incorporates the origin of key religious elements such as the Sabbath and the categorical basis for Jewish dietary regulations.

The role of the human in this well-ordered recital is sort of like that of a priest. Like a priest who passes on tradition, presides over the order of worship, and is the agent of God, so was the human to be a steward of the mysteries of creation, to witness to and act on behalf of the divine Presence. This is where we get our concept of humanity being given a unique function—dominion—in the world.

Of course, it is easy to see how this notion of dominion has gotten bent into unrecognizable shape. At best, humans have seen themselves as "better than" the rest of the world. At worst, creation has been seen as a slave, available to fulfill every whim of humanity.

Yet while humans may have been charged with a unique function in the world, they did not get a unique essence. All life comes from God, who made it out of the dust of the ground (Gen. 2:7, 19). And our job is to be *God's* representatives, not our own interests. We are to "control" the land only in the way God, the loving creator, might do. As well, Christ's model of dominion as servant suggests we are to care for creation so that it sustains all. As Christians, we are called to make sure that we use the earth in keeping with God's loving intent, not our own will.

In Session 3 of this unit, we will encounter another account of creation with a different twist: from Genesis 2. This version gives humans not so much a priestly role in creation, but a servant role. While in Genesis 1 humans are called to "subdue," or master, creation, the charge in Genesis 2 is for humans to "cultivate," literally, *to serve the soil*. This places human labor under the *land's* control. Most farmers will probably tell you that's just how farming feels; to have one's life run by concern for the land.

But the most common Christian basis of humanity's relationship to the rest of creation has been neither of these Genesis accounts, but the view of the Apostle Paul, which regards nature as fallen and in need of redemption. There is also the presumption that this earth will pass away and be replaced by a new creation. Such a view makes it easy to take the small leap toward exploitation of the earth's resources (since it's all going to end anyway), as well as seeing ourselves as striving to be completely divorced from "baser" nature.

"We are not God. The Earth was here before us and was given to us."

Pope Francis, *On Care for Our Common Home*, 67.

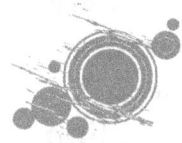

>>> LOOK AHEAD

For one of next session's Focus options, you'll need serving-size boxes of a variety of dry cereals (or make your own servings in plastic bags). Hand out copies of the reader's theatre to three people so they can practice during the week. Also, locate addresses for writing letters if you would like to use that option in Respond.

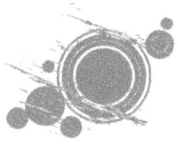

> **"'Let us worship the Lord in the beauty of holiness,' says the psalm. What is beauty? Beauty is a sum not reducible to its parts. It is a perception of harmony in variety. What is worship? To worship means not to figure out, not to analyze, not to pin down like a dried butterfly on a grid, but to value. Deeply to value."**
>
> William Bryant Logan, *Dirt: The Ecstatic Skin of the Earth*

But that's not God's original intention, and Paul was not focused on environmental dilemmas, especially the kind we experience today. The two Genesis accounts leave us a different ethos, and a different mandate. Both stories highlight the sacredness of the universe which God created, and invite us to live in harmony with creation. In the words of Pope Francis, we are invited to "regain the conviction that we need one another, that we have a shared responsibility for others and the world." (*On Care for Our Common Home*, 229)

If we believe that God made the world, we do not need any reason to hold and protect creation other than that God is embedded in this treasure.

Exploring tough questions facing youth today

Crammin' about Creation

Characters: **Fimmy Jallon**—A typical talk-show host
Sarah—Bible scholar (*holds a Bible*)

(*Sarah starts off-stage, with an empty seat for her at front of room. Fimmy stands, perhaps using a pen for a microphone.*)

Fimmy Jallon: Welcome, everyone, to the newest show about something as old as the earth itself, "Crammin' about Creation." I'm your host, Fimmy Jallon!

Today we have a very special guest who is ready to answer questions about the very origins of the world itself! She's a Bible scholar, and a specialist in the Dead Sea Scrolls. Please give a warm welcome to Sarah McMalachi! (*Sarah enters.*)

Welcome, Sarah! (*Make small talk about weather, etc.*) Well, everyone's dying to hear what you have to say about the very beginnings of the world, Sarah, and see what light the Good Book sheds on the issue. Our first question has stumped scientists for generations. Sarah, maybe you can set us straight: *When* was the universe created?

SARAH: Yes, well, I'm terribly sorry to disappoint you, but I can't say exactly how many years ago or anything like that. The author of the story wasn't worried about such details, and so the Bible doesn't give an exact date. It does, however, give us an answer. It's right here in Genesis 1:1. (*Choose someone from the audience to read the passage.*) I suppose, then, the answer would be, in the beginning. On a Monday, perhaps.

FJ: Ah,...yes, "the beginning" just about covers it, doesn't it? Can't really argue with that. Let's move on to our next question. Sarah, *who* created the world?

SARAH: Well, if you'd been listening before, the passage that was read said that in the beginning GOD created the heavens and the earth! That pretty much sums it up right there!

FJ: Sorry, thanks for refreshing our memories.... On to the next question: *How* was everything created?

SARAH: Well, all we know from Genesis 1 is that God said, and it was so. Let's read it. (*Choose youth to read Genesis 1:2-31, with each person reading one day of creation.*) So, to answer the question we can say that God made the earth with purpose. God began with chaos and unfolded an ordered world, complete with plants, animals, and people. All the Bible tells us is that God told it to happen, and it did.

FJ: Well, now, it's time for the final question for our esteemed scholar. Sarah, *why* was the world created?

SARAH: I suppose the first answer is to fill the earth with life. Genesis 1 tells us that God made every kind of plant, swarms of fish and birds, and every kind of animal. Then, of course, God tells them to go and do that...that fruitful and multiply thing.

Second, we read that the earth is to provide for the needs of life—God interconnects plants, animals, and people so that life may continue.

Third, we read that God got to the end of the work, stood back, so to speak, and said, "This is really good!" So God must have wanted to create something...good!

FJ: So there you have it, folks—the when, who, how and why of creation. Tune in next time when we'll have a live interview with an orchardist from Washington who can trace her family tree all the way back to Adam and Eve! Good-bye, everyone, and may the good earth sustain you!

Permission is granted to photocopy this handout for use with this session.

Unit affirmation

> We care for the earth because:
>
> God made it;
>
> God owns it;
>
> God cares for it;
>
> God wills it;
>
> God speaks through it;
>
> God acts in it.
>
> Shantilal Bhagat, in "God's Earth Our Home."

>>>

All-powerful God,

you are present in the whole universe and in the smallest of your creatures. You embrace with your tenderness all that exists. Pour out upon us the power of your love, that we may protect life and beauty. AMEN

Pope Francis, *On Care for Our Common Home*, 246.

Explore: For great ideas on individual and group projects that make a difference, check out New Community Project (NewCommunityProject.org) and YES magazine online (YesMagazine.org).

Permission is granted to photocopy this handout for use with this session.

>>> **SESSION 2**

BABBLINGS ON BABEL >>>

>> KEY VERSE

Therefore it was called Babel, because there the Lord confused the language of all the earth; and from there the Lord scattered them abroad over the face of all the earth. (Gen. 11:9)

>> FAITH STORY

Genesis 11:1-9

>> FAITH FOCUS

The descendants of Noah had received God's blessing to multiply and fill the earth. Instead, the people gathered into one place and found their own goal to live for: a tower reaching high into the heavens. But God responded by mixing up their languages, scattering them over the earth, and giving the human race some much-needed diversity. God created a variety of life, and values differences in plants, animals, and people.

>> SESSION GOAL

Develop in participants the desire to protect the variety God intends for creation.

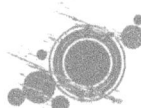

TEACHING PLAN

>> **Materials needed and advance preparation**

- Pencils/pens and writing paper
- Varieties of dry cereal, milk, spoons (see Focus *Option A*)
- Three copies of handout sheet for Session 2; give to three readers ahead of time, if possible
- Ball of yarn
- Addresses and materials for writing letters (see Respond *Option A*)
- Materials for a wall mural (see Respond *Option C*)

1. FOCUS 4-8 minutes

This activity starts participants thinking about the value of variety and diversity.

>> **Option A:** Divide into two groups, and have breakfast! Hand one group a bag filled with a variety of dry cereals (either small variety-pack boxes or small plastic bags each with about a serving of cereal). Give the other group another bag filled with cereal, but just **one** kind (either small boxes of all cornflakes or some such, or small plastic bags with about a serving each). Allow the group with a variety of cereals to trade among themselves, if they wish. No trading across group lines.

Have a breakfast blessing, then point out milk and spoons and eat (right out of the boxes or plastic bags!). Deal with any grumbling by saying, *We'll talk about it after we finish eating.*

Go to Connect, *Option A*.

>> **Option B:** Hand out two sheets of paper and a pencil/pen to each person. Let them know that you are going ask them to draw an object on each sheet of paper. Tell them these are not meant to be works of art; you are only going to give them 10 seconds for each picture. First, ask them to draw a tree, then a flower. Everyone should keep their drawing to themselves. Collect the papers so they can be anonymously displayed.

Go to Connect, *Option B*.

>> **Option C:** (for camp or retreat setting):

For one meal, serve just one item, and plenty of it. Use the experience to discuss what it would be like to have little or no variety in the world.

Go to Explore the Bible.

2. CONNECT 3-4 minutes

>> **Option A:** Ask for a show of hands of all those who were satisfied with their breakfast. Discuss why they were happy, then give anyone who didn't raise a hand a chance to complain. Use the experience to discuss what it would be like to have little or no variety in the world.

>> **Option B:** As a group, examine the drawings. How many different types of trees can you see in the pictures? How many types of flowers? How do the drawings reflect the trees and flowers around your area?

When we think of a tree or flower, we tend to have certain shapes and characteristics in our minds. We tend to lump all evergreen trees together into a Christmas tree shape, and all flowers into daisies or tulips. There are over 250,000 flowering plants in the world, of all different shapes and sizes. There are also thousands of species of trees. Discuss briefly why we tend to think of the same images for a tree or flower when there are so many different kinds.

Shift to the next activity by saying: *God created the earth and filled it with variety; a wide assortment of trees, plants, and animals. But humans sometimes work against God's desire for variety. Here's a time when "getting it together" blew God's stack.*

3. EXPLORE THE BIBLE 10-12 minutes

Introduce the story of the Tower of Babel:

According to Genesis 1, the Creator made humans, blessed them, and called them to "fill the earth." After the Great Flood, God repeated this blessing to Noah and his descendants. But in Genesis 11, we find that Noah's great-great-great-grandchildren have resisted God's calling. Let's listen.

Present the story of the Tower of Babel using:

>> **Option A:** The "Babblings on Babel" (Reader's Theatre) handout sheet.

>> **Option B:** The "Towers of Babel during Chaldean Empire AKA Neo-Babylonian Empire" video on YouTube (https://youtu.be/zvSUM5BMxgg).

>> **For Both Options:**

The descendants of Noah had unified themselves under one purpose. The problem was that in doing so, they ignored God's intention for them. When God changed the language of the people, it was not as much a punishment as a way of making sure that God's plan to fill the earth with diversity was carried out. Discuss the Bible passage:

- *Why do you think the people didn't want to be scattered?*
- *How would you feel if you were forced to leave your friends and relatives and move to a different country?*
- *Why do you think the people decided to build a tower?*
- *What do you think would have happened if one person had stepped out of line and refused to help build the tower? Or if a few decided to build their own tower?*

4. APPLY 15-20 minutes

Explain that by separating and going their different ways, the people of Babel opened themselves to a variety of ideas and purposes, in keeping with God's intention. With different languages, people were able to develop a variety of different cultures and ways of doing things.

Divide into two groups, and have a culture contest. Give each group two minutes to write down on a sheet of paper things we enjoy that come from other cultures and countries. See who can come up with the most things.

Some examples would be:

- Italian food (spaghetti—originally from China!—and pizza!)
- Bach, Beethoven, Shakespeare, and Handel's *Messiah*
- music groups like Coldplay, Five SOS, Little Mix
- "O Come, O Come, Emmanuel," "Angels We Have Heard on High," "What Child is This?" and "Silent Night"
- Hondas, Ferraris, and bicycles

Share the two lists. Imagine what your world would be like without these things!

Shift to natural diversity with something like the following: *Differences are also important in nature. The variety and diversity make it interesting and exciting. It also makes survival possible. But even in its variety, all life is connected, and each organism plays an important role.*

>> Option A: This activity can take place outside. Ask the group to stand and form a circle. Hold up a ball of yarn, and explain that you are going to make a "Web of Life" to show how elements in the natural world are connected to each other.

Say that you represent sunlight, sending energy into the environment. Ask: *What gets its food from sunlight?* Encourage specific answers, like grass or trees. Hold on to your end of the yarn as you pass the ball across to a second person who represents tree. Ask: *What gets its food from trees or fruit?* Continue in this pattern until everyone is holding on to the yarn and there is a crisscross pattern in the middle of the group.

Guide people's suggestions to develop an adequate chain. Here's an example for how the order might be worked out:

Sunlight	Bobcat	Fly (lay eggs on Hawk's dead carcass)
Tree	Tick	
Aphid	Frog	Pheasant
Wasp	Snake	Human
Blue Jay	Hawk	

UNIT AFFIRMATION

We care for the earth because:

God made it;

God owns it;

God cares for it;

God wills it;

God speaks through it;

God acts in it.

Shantilal Bhagat, in "God's Earth Our Home."

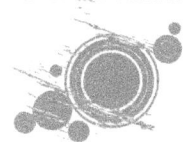

> "Look hard at ecosystems to see what's at the bottom of their replication, cleanup, and maintenance—the crucial domestic labor of a planet, the grunt work that keeps everything else alive. That is: soil microbes, keystone predators, marine invertebrates, pollinating insects, and phytoplankton."
>
> Barbara Kingsolver, *Small Wonder*

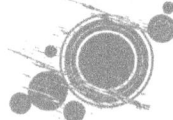

LOOK AHEAD

Locate a stuffed animal for next session's Focus activity.

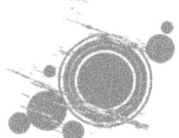

Debrief the Web of Life you have created through the following:

1. Say to the group that pollution is hurting one member of the food web (e.g., acid rain hurting the frog). Have that person pull on their end of the yarn. *Who feels the pull? What happens to the rest of the web? How might this represent what happens when one member of the ecosystem experiences stress or its survival is threatened?*

2. Announce that you are going to chop down the tree. Instruct everyone to drop their end of the yarn when the thing they eat is no longer a part of the web. *What happens to the web? What does this tell us about the effect one action can have on an entire ecosystem?*

3. If time permits, build a second Web of Life using only three people. Repeat steps 1 and 2. *How strongly do the members of the web feel the pull? Are there any members that do not feel a strong pull? How long does it take for the web to fall completely apart once the tree is cut down? What might this tell us about the stability of an ecosystem?*

>> **Option B:** (for camp or retreat setting):

Divide into groups of six, if possible. Ask each person to pick a specific plant, animal, or organism for themselves. Now, attempt to build a human pyramid with the plants on the bottom, herbivores in the middle, and carnivores on top. *Are your pyramids balanced? Do they work at all?* Explain that pyramids only work if they are balanced. The same is true in the natural world. We need a large number of plants on the bottom, a smaller number of herbivores in the middle, and only one or two carnivores on top. Have each group reassign themselves so they can build a balanced pyramid.

>> **For Both Options:** Summarize the experience by making the following points:

- *When God works towards variety and diversity in the ecosystem, God ensures that creation is balanced and able to adjust to the pressures that might be placed on it.*
- *We as humans are a part of the ecosystem. When we put stress on our environment, not only do we put stress on the rest of the ecosystem, but on ourselves as well.*
- *We threaten the diversity of the ecosystem when we:*
  - *view nature only in terms of monetary value.*
  - *threaten species with extinction.*
  - *destroy habitats that we humans do not find useful.*

5. RESPOND 5-10 minutes

>> **Option A:** Write letters of support to environmental projects that are working to preserve biodiversity. Examples include:

- *government habitat protection programs*
- *species re-introduction (e.g., wolves to Yellowstone park)*
- *species preservation (e.g., Royal Botanic Gardens, at Kew, London, or the Plant Genetics Resources Unit in Geneva, NY, that works to preserve disappearing plant species)*

Conclude with the unit affirmation printed on page 13 (or on the handout sheet).

>> **Option B:** Say: *God has created an incredible variety of life here on earth. Each one of us is an example of that variety. We all have something unique to contribute to this group, to the church, and to the world.*

Ask the group to consider each member one at a time. As a group, come up with one or two things that are special or unique about each person. Together as a group, think of one thing that each person can do to help preserve the variety in your church or in creation.

End in prayer, thanking God for the variety that exists in creation and asking God to help us protect the diversity that exists in nature and each other. Conclude with the unit affirmation printed on page 13 (or on the handout sheet).

>> **Option C:** Construct a mural with as many different kinds of animals, plants, landscapes, seeds, etc. as possible. These can either be drawn, or named. Give the mural an appropriate title (e.g., "The Diversity of Creation"), and hang it in the foyer of your church building. Close with the unit affirmation on page 13 (or on the handout sheet).

INSIGHTS FROM SCRIPTURE

At first glance, the story of the Tower of Babel sounds like a fable explaining the origins of different languages. A closer look reveals that the story is not as concerned with language as it is with scattering. The spreading of life over the earth is an important theme in the early chapters of Genesis. God intentionally made a variety of creatures, and wanted them to "be fruitful and multiply" (Gen. 1:22), filling the earth, sea, and sky.

This same command is given to humanity; humans, also, are to fill the earth, bringing a healthy relationship with God and creation to every corner of the world. Just as the Genesis 1 creation story is an account of ordering by separation (light from dark, water from land), so is this a story of separating, of scattering.

>> NOAH'S DESCENDANTS

After the flood, God started over. In Genesis 9:1, God repeated the blessing of multiplying and filling the earth, reaffirming the desire for an earth full of life. But when Genesis brings us to the Plain of Shinar, we find that the descendants of Noah have resisted God's will. They settled in one place, ignoring God's command to spread. They feared being scattered and actually worked to prevent it (Gen. 11:4). The people did not fear punishment; they feared the very purpose for which God created them.

The people gathered into one place because they wished to reach their own goals. They resisted God's command (Gen. 11:4) by building a tower, a united effort to glorify their own name and not God's. They relied on their numbers, their technology (Gen. 11:3), their city, and their tower. They ignored their God.

God did not let this lack of faith go unchallenged. Though the people at Babel saw it as punishment, God responded in such a way as to ensure that people bring forth the variety and diversity that was intended.

"Wilderness... had to be saved because it was one of the last pure places where an individual with open eyes and a clean heart could experience the sense of community that the first man and woman had experienced before the fall. Muir believed that in the wilderness God still walked perceptibly among the inhabitants of his garden, who submitted to one another under the law of love. If it was destroyed, not only would many conscious and sentient creatures suffer and die, but mankind [sic] might lose the last great prophet."

Dennis Williams, "The Spiritual Value of Nature," in *John Muir, Life and Work*

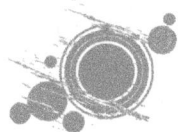

UNITED BY FAITH IN GOD

God desires unity of spirit, but a unified purpose outside of God's intentions quickly becomes oppressive. In such an atmosphere, no person can be uniquely herself. A dramatic example of this is Nazi Germany in the 1940s, but it also exists in our own society when national purposes become so important that any independent thought is seen as a threat to the united goals. Teenagers today experience this to a certain extent in the form of peer pressure. The range of self-expression is limited by what one's friends or society can accept.

God delights in the vast diversity of life in creation. We need only look at the wide variety of species of animals and plants within creation to see that God has a great imagination. Participants can strengthen their connection to the variety in God's creation first by appreciating it, simply because it is God's, and then by protecting it.

Babblings on Babel

A three-voice Reader's Theatre based on Genesis 11:1-9.

Reader 1: Now the whole earth had one language and the same words.
Reader 2: Now the whole earth had one language and the same words.
Reader 3: Now the whole earth had one language and the same words.
Reader 1: And as the descendants of Noah migrated from the east,
Reader 2: they came upon a plain in the land of Shinar,
Reader 3: and they settled there.
Reader 1: And they said to one another,
Reader 3: "Come, let us make bricks, and bake them thoroughly."
Reader 2: And they used brick
Reader 1: instead of stone
Reader 3: And they used tar
Reader 1: instead of mortar.
Reader 2: Then they said,
Reader 1: "Come, let us build ourselves a city, and a tower with its top in the heavens, and let us make a name for ourselves; otherwise we shall be scattered abroad over the face of the whole earth."
Reader 2: scattered abroad
Reader 3: scattered
Reader 2: The Lord came down to see the city and the tower that the people were building.
Reader 1: And the Lord said,
Reader 2: "Look, they are one people, and they have all one language; and this is only the beginning of what they will do; nothing they try to do will be impossible for them. Come, let us go down, and confuse their language so that they will not able to understand each other."
Reader 3: So the Lord scattered them abroad.
Reader 1: scattered them abroad
Reader 2: scattered
Reader 1: over the face of all the earth.
Reader 3: Therefore the place was called Babel,
Reader 2: because there the Lord confused the language of all the earth;
Reader 1: And from there the Lord scattered them abroad
Reader 3: scattered them abroad
Reader 2: scattered
Reader 3: over the face of all the earth.

Permission is granted to photocopy this handout for use with this session.

SESSION 3

WHAT'S IN A NAME?

KEY VERSE

So out of the ground the Lord God formed every animal of the field and every bird of the air, and brought them to the man to see what he would call them; and whatever the man called every living creature, that was its name. (Gen. 2:19)

FAITH STORY

Genesis 2:4b-9, 15-23

FAITH FOCUS

The Genesis 2 account of creation is concerned primarily with humanity and its place in the world. The passage recognizes a strong kinship between humanity and every other living thing in the garden since they are all made out of the ground. The connection is also recognized in the vocation given to humanity. The task of naming invokes an integral, caring relationship between humanity and the environment.

SESSION GOAL

Help participants realize that their relationship to the rest of creation, and especially to God, obligates them to care for God's world.

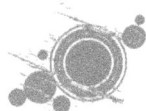

TEACHING PLAN

Materials needed and advance preparation

- A stuffed animal (see Focus *Option A*)
- Slips of paper with names of animals, one per person (see Focus *Option B*)
- Blindfold
- Copies of handout sheet for Session 3
- Pencil/pen, writing paper
- Bibles
- Chalkboard/chalk or newsprint/markers

1. FOCUS 8-12 minutes

Option A: Pass the stuffed animal around so everyone gets a chance to handle it. Say something like, *I brought this here today because I'd like some help choosing a suitable name.* Discuss names for the toy. If the toy belongs to someone special, or is destined to become the group mascot, this will add meaning to the naming.

Start participants thinking about what a name represents. Say: *Each of you has probably named a pet or toy. Let's hear some stories of why you chose the name you did.* Perhaps people have a funny story to tell surrounding names. Example: Because he pawed at the piano, we named the dog Beethoven.

In Real Life | Keeping the Garden 25

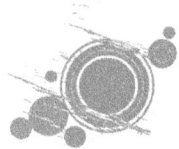

YOUTH TODAY

Questions of conservation and protection of the environment are often pitted against immediate economic needs. Does it come down to a choice between the lives of animals and plants and the livelihoods of people? Threatened with environmental and population crises, youth ask how to walk the line between the needs of the environment and the needs of people.

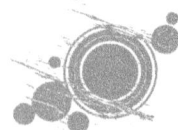

"The climate is a common good, belonging to all and meant for all."

Pope Francis, *On Care for Our Common Home*, 23.

>>> **Option B:** (for camp or retreat setting):

Play Zookeeper. Draft one person to be the zookeeper, and hand everyone else a slip of paper with the name of an animal written on it. Keep the names secret. Point out that the entire playing area is the zoo, and all the animals are contained in it. The zookeeper is responsible for protecting the animals, which are all endangered species.

But one of the animals escapes the cage at night and the rest of the zoo goes crazy! Blindfold the zookeeper, and silently designate one of the "animals" to be the escapee, while the rest of the animals spread out in the room or playing area. Then signal all players to *loudly* make the sound of the animal on their paper. . The zookeeper, meanwhile, has 30-45 seconds (a little more time for larger groups) to tag and *name* the designated animal, who may move around slowly. Whenever the zookeeper calls "Who are you?" the "escapee" must always answer with an animal sound. When named, the animal must sit down and stop making sounds. Continue until all animals have been named.

Alternative: Play in the dark, allowing animals to roam around, and no blindfold on the zookeeper.
(game adapted from *Screamers and Scramblers*, Michael W. Capps)

2. CONNECT 5-7 minutes

Names are very important. Explain that generally when you name something you expect to be in contact with it, learn something about it. Example: If you lived on a poultry farm you probably *wouldn't* name chickens you were going to eat!

Say: *Imagine you've discovered a new species of animal. How would you go about naming it?* (a name to describe its appearance? to describe the discoverer? to describe where it came from?) *What would you want people to know about it as soon as they see the name? How would you feel about this discovery if you could verify that there were only 100 of these animals in the world?*

When you name something, you expect it to be around for a while. You open yourself to a relationship, and you care about how it's treated and what happens to it.

Shift to the next activity by saying: *God created the world, but left it to Adam to name the creatures. God intended that people have some sort of caring relationship to creation. Let's look at another creation story from Genesis 2.*

3. EXPLORE THE BIBLE 12-17 minutes

>>> **Option A:** Divide into 3 groups, and distribute handout sheets. Assign each group one of the Bible passages and accompanying questions. Ask them to record answers to share with the entire group.

Group 1: Genesis 1:26-30

1. What role in the environment are humans given?
2. What does Mark 9:33-35 say about what it means to be great?
3. How do we understand dominion over the earth in Genesis 1 in light of Jesus' teachings of what it means to be great?

Group 2: Genesis 2:4b-9, 18-19

1. What did God create plants, animals, and humans out of? What does this suggest about the relationship between humanity and the rest of creation?
2. What two qualities did plants possess when they were created? What does this suggest about the role creation is to play in relationship to humanity?

26   In Real Life | Keeping the Garden

Group 3: Genesis 2:15-23

1. What jobs did God give Adam? (See especially verses 15 and 19.)
2. How could naming nature in a descriptive way help with the tasks of tilling and keeping creation?

After 5-6 minutes, call the groups back together. Ask each group to explain their passage, questions, and answers with the rest of the group. Take a few moments to discuss interesting points.

》》 Option B: Divide into two groups, and distribute handout sheets. Assign each group one of the perspectives under "Debate."

Team 1: God made the earth for people to use. When we use the earth's resources we are simply filling the role God designed for us. Being made in the image of God makes us representatives of God in the world. Besides, Jesus said that this world will come to an end anyway. There are more important human concerns than spending our energy preserving a world destined to be replaced by a new creation.

Team 2: The environment exists for more than just our personal use. God values all of creation, and calls it good. God allows us to use its resources to fulfill our needs, but we must not threaten its ability to meet the needs of people for generations to come. Besides, God has purposes for nature that we cannot fully understand. We need to take care of God's earth and make sure we live in a healthy relationship with it.

Instruct each group to read Genesis 1:26-31, 2:4b-9, and 15-23 in light of their assigned perspectives. Then give the teams 3-4 minutes to ready arguments for debate. You may want to check in with each team and offer assistance if needed.

Give each team one minute to present its case. Then, give both sides one or two 30-second opportunities for rebuttal. Allow each group a closing statement.

Debrief using the following questions:

1. *Did you find it easy to debate from your assigned perspective? Why or why not?*
2. *Which of the arguments comes closest to the way our faith community tends to view Christian relationship to the environment?*

4. APPLY 9-10 minutes

Give a 2-3-minute mini-lecture with the following points:

- The two accounts of creation in Genesis give us two pictures of the human role in creation. In Genesis 1, humans have been assigned by God to a powerful, managerial role in creation; they are stewards. But in Genesis 2, the first human was commissioned to cultivate, literally "to serve" the soil. These two images present the paradox of human existence. On one hand, we humans are, of all species, uniquely powerful and inventive. On the other hand, our very survival is dependent on biological, chemical, and geological processes we hardly understand, let alone control.
- Humanity is intricately connected with its environment. When we damage the environment, we endanger our very survival.
- Our society often considers only the value of money. How much can nature earn for us? But we also need to consider the earth's aesthetic value, recreational value, and its future value. What may be seen as useless to us today might be very important down the road. **Example:** Rain forest plants are an important source of medicines, yet we have tested less than 10% of them! Instead, forests are destroyed to drill for more and more oil we think we need currently or to raise cattle for more and cheaper red meat that buyers are demanding.

》》 UNIT AFFIRMATION

We care for the earth because:

God made it;

God owns it;

God cares for it;

God wills it;

God speaks through it;

God acts in it.

Shantilal Bhagat, in "God's Earth Our Home."

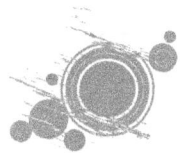

>>> LOOK AHEAD

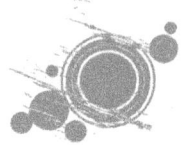

Check for the rather odd assortment of materials you'll need for next session's Focus activity. Also, if you are planning on the quilt option in Apply, gather the necessary materials.

>>>

"I do not know whether it is possible to love the planet or not, but I do know that it is possible to love the places we can see, touch, smell, and experience."

David Orr, *Earth in Mind*

- We also don't always know the effect of our actions on the environment. An activity thought to be harmless now can have serious repercussions down the road. Technology doesn't always have the answer. **Example:** In the late 1800s, a newspaper in Toronto reported a growing concern with the problem of horse manure on city streets. It predicted that if current increases in horse travel continued, it would not be long before the city would be 4 feet deep in horse manure! Cars were a miracle solution—transportation with no waste to shovel! Today the smog over cities tells us all too clearly that cars indeed have waste!

Conclude your talk with something like the following: *We need to live in a healthy relationship with the environment and use its resources in ways that make sure it continues to provide for life in the future. By caring for the environment, through tilling and keeping, we fulfill God's call. We cannot do whatever we want with the environment. We must name ourselves properly as* **servants** *to God's creation.*

Write down a list of common persons, places, or things that impact the lives of youth. As a group, "name" these things for what they do in our lives. List positive and negative influences. Write on a chalkboard or newsprint so everyone can see. For example:

	Positive Names	**Negative Names**
Car	transportation	smog producer, fuel guzzler, status symbol
Music Star	entertainer, artist	idol, excessive lifestyle example, resource drain
Clothing	cover, warmth	status symbol, allowance eliminator
Rain forest	oxygen producer, climate stabilizer, wildlife haven	money producer, pasture encroacher

By "naming" the influences these things have on us, we gain the ability to do something about them. When I refer to my car as a smog producer, I acknowledge an awareness of a problem. The next time I go to use my "smog producer," perhaps I will decide to use alternative transportation instead.

5. RESPOND 7-10 minutes

>> **Option A:** As a group, look at both the positive and negative names you came up with in Apply. Add a third column entitled, "Our Pledge to Care for Creation." Fill this column, keeping in mind God's command to till and keep the earth. Encourage each person to commit themselves to some/all of these changes in the coming weeks.

Close in prayer, asking God for the wisdom to name the world in ways that fulfill our obligation to "till and keep" God's creation. End with the unit affirmation.

>> **Option B:** When we look at naming the world for what it truly is, we are asking ourselves to take a look at things from perspectives other than our own. How would the Genesis 2 creation story be different if it were written from the point of view of a deer? A tree? Someone in a less developed country?

Divide into groups of 2-4. Ask each group to write the creation story from the perspective of a plant or animal. Give 5 minutes to come up with their story, then spend the remainder of the time sharing and discussing your stories.

Close in prayer, asking God for the wisdom to name the world in ways that fulfill our obligation to "till and keep" God's creation. End with the unit affirmation.

 INSIGHTS FROM SCRIPTURE

The two accounts of creation in Genesis give us two pictures of the human role in creation. In Genesis 1, humans have been assigned by God to a powerful, managerial role in creation; they are stewards. But in Genesis 2, the first human was commissioned to cultivate, literally "to serve" the soil. These two images present the paradox of human existence. On one hand, we humans are, of all species, uniquely powerful and inventive. On the other hand, our very survival is dependent on biological, chemical, and geological processes we hardly understand, let alone control.

The Genesis 2 passage also makes several important points about creation and its relationship with humanity:

1. **A strong kinship exists between humanity and the rest of the life in creation.** Every living thing shares the same parentage, and owes its existence to the same Creator, who brought them all into being out of the same raw material—"dust of the ground" (vv. 7, 9, 19)—and provided each of them with direction and purpose.

2. **God intends humanity and the rest of creation to share a close relationship.** First, creation provides for human need (vv. 9a, 16). This not only includes the physical need for food, but also the hunger for beauty and refreshment. Too often our society reduces nature to its monetary value, and ignores the aesthetic, medicinal, mental, and future value of creation.

God also intended creation to provide for Adam's need of companionship. Even though no suitable helper or partner was found among the animals created in 2:19, the passage states that God created these beings with companionship in mind.

In response to these gifts of relationship, humanity is to serve creation. Humans are entrusted with care of the garden, and given two important tasks: to "till it and keep it" (Gen. 2:15). These tasks are agricultural in nature, and suggest a gardener or a shepherd. Tilling is not a license for extracting as much as possible from the earth. We are to work with the earth to enhance its God-given purposes.

Humans are also to "keep" creation. "Keeping" suggests nurturing creation to function for the long term. Native and aboriginal peoples traditionally see current actions and attitudes as affecting "seven generations" into the future. By keeping creation, humans are to ensure that it continues to produce, thrive, and fulfill its purposes for generations to come.

> "There is in biology a formula called 'the equation of burning'... [which]... describes how plants (and animals) unlock the stored sunlight and turn it into the heat energy that fuels their motion, their feeling, their thought, or whatever their living consists of.... All that is living burns. This is the fundamental fact of nature. And Moses saw it with his two eyes, directly. That glimpse of the real world—of the world as it is known to God—is not a world of isolate things, but of processes in concert."
>
> William Bryant Logan,
> *Dirt: The Ecstatic Skin of the Earth*

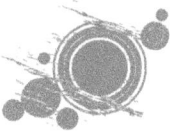

›› THE GIFT OF NAMING

The passage identifies one very important ability humans have to help them till and keep the garden: the ability to name. When we name something, we expect to have a relationship with it. We tend not to name animals we are going to eat, but we name pets with which we expect to interact.

Naming has incredible power. By naming, humans provide order to the world. When we name something, it defines the relationship existing between us. By naming creation, we designate how we view other life and how we can use it. The name we give something reflects our understanding of its purpose, and its relationship with us.

God calls us to name the world appropriately. We need to look at the earth's natural resources and name them for what they really are. When we look at a forest, we could consider the value in the lumber and name it "money." Instead, God calls us to consider *all* of its characteristics and importance. We must recognize its other names: "animal habitat," "oxygen producer," "water collector," and "beautiful."

›› UNIQUE FUNCTION, NOT UNIQUE ESSENCE

Humans possess capacities different from any other creature on earth. God created us with a unique function in the world, and we can thus affect the environment in major ways. We have the power to till, to harvest the resources of the earth. We have the power to name, to order things.

But humans do not have a unique essence in creation. Being related to all living things, we are instructed to till the garden in such a way that its life-giving capacity is not diminished. We are to enjoy the aesthetic and spiritual value of life, not just the monetary value. We are to order our way of living in such a way that it does not threaten to return God's creation to chaos. We are to care for the garden, to enhance all aspects of the ecosystem, and to ensure that it keeps providing for life.

It's all about perspective!

In Real Life — Exploring tough questions facing youth today

The two accounts of creation in Genesis give us two pictures of the human role in creation. On one hand, we humans are, of all species, uniquely powerful and inventive. On the other hand, our very survival is dependent on biological, chemical, and geological processes we hardly understand, let alone control.

Group 1: Genesis 1:26-30
1. What role in the environment are humans given?
2. What does Mark 9:33-35 say about what it means to be great?
3. How do we understand dominion over the earth in Genesis 1 in light of Jesus' teachings of what it means to be great?

Group 2: Genesis 2:4b-9, 18-19
1. What did God create plants, animals, and humans out of? What does this suggest about the relationship between humanity and the rest of creation?
2. What two qualities did plants possess when they were created? What does this suggest about the role creation is to play in relationship to humanity?

Group 3: Genesis 2:15-23
1. What jobs did God give Adam? (See especially verses 15 and 19.)
2. How could naming nature in a descriptive way help with the tasks of tilling and keeping creation?

DEBATE!

Whether or not you agree with it, you have been assigned a perspective, below: With your team, prepare your case using Genesis 1:26-31, 2:4b-9, and 15-23; each team will have one minute to present, a 30-second rebuttal period, and a closing statement.

Team 1: God made the earth for people to use. When we use the earth's resources we are simply filling the role God designed for us. Being made in the image of God makes us representatives of God in the world. Besides, Jesus said that this world will come to an end anyway. There are more important human concerns than spending our energy preserving a world destined to be replaced by a new creation.

Team 2: The environment exists for more than just our personal use. God values all of creation, and calls it good. God allows us to use its resources to fulfill our needs, but we must not threaten its ability to meet the needs of people for generations to come. Besides, God has purposes for nature that we cannot fully understand. We need to take care of God's earth and make sure we live in a healthy relationship with it.

Keeping the Garden : Session 3

Permission is granted to photocopy this handout for use with this session.

>>> **SESSION 4**

PUSHING GOD'S 'LEGAL LIMITS' >>>

>>> KEY VERSES

The woman said to the serpent, "We may eat of the fruit of the trees in the garden; but God said, 'You shall not eat of the fruit of the tree that is in the middle of the garden, nor shall you touch it,
or you shall die.'" (Gen. 3:2-3)

>>> FAITH STORY

Genesis 3:1-19

>>> FAITH FOCUS

When God placed humans in the Garden of Eden, they were allowed to eat the fruit of many trees, and forbidden to eat of only one. But then they ignored this one limitation. Our covenant with God establishes limits on human behavior, but when we refuse to accept those limits, the whole world suffers.

>>> SESSION GOAL

Encourage participants to live within the limits of creation.

>>> Materials needed and advance preparation

- One six-sided die, knife and fork, oven mitts, and a chocolate bar wrapped with several layers of newspaper and masking tape (see Focus Option A)
- Materials for the game of your choice (see Focus Option B)
- Bibles
- Pencils/pens and paper
- Rulers or straightedges for each person
- Box full of garbage (see Apply Option B)
- Large sheets of paper/posterboard, markers, etc., for making pledge posters
- Rags/scraps/old clothes for quilt (see Apply Option C)

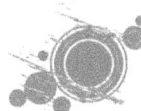

TEACHING PLAN

1. FOCUS 6-8 minutes

>>> **Option A:** Ask the group to sit in a circle on the floor. In the middle, place the wrapped chocolate bar, a pair of oven mitts, a knife, and a fork.

Take turns rolling the die. The first person to roll a six rushes to the middle, puts on the oven mitts, and attempts to unwrap and eat the chocolate bar using only the knife and fork. The other participants continue rolling. When a second person rolls a six, the first person must stop and hand over the oven mitts and cutlery. The next person now has a chance to see how far they get.

For a time, continue to play the game as described above. Once two or three people have managed to get some chocolate, announce loudly that there are no more rules. See what happens!

In Real Life | Keeping the Garden 33

>> **Option B:** Select a simple game for members of your group to play (e.g., jacks, marbles, tic-tac-toe, cards such as "Old Maid," "Uno," "Go Fish"). Play it for a few minutes, then announce that there are no more rules. See what happens!

2. CONNECT 5-6 minutes

Briefly discuss the outcome of the game. Ask questions like:

- *What happened to the game once the rules were removed?*
- *Was the game more enjoyable with rules, or without rules? Why?*

Ask the group to get comfortable and close their eyes. Tell them to let their imaginations run wild as you read two situations. After each reading, briefly discuss the questions following.

Situation 1. Imagine you are driving a car on a busy city street. You're on your way to the concert of a lifetime, with the best tickets in the house. Yet traffic is horribly slow, and you realize that at this rate you will be late. Imagine there are suddenly no traffic laws—no speed limits, red lights mean nothing, and it doesn't matter which side of the road you're on.

- *What would you do?*
- *What would happen at the next busy intersection?*

Say: *Limits are important. Imagine what life and society would be like if there were no limits!*

Situation 2. You are at a crowded mall shopping for new clothes. You really need new jeans, but the only pair you like is way out of your price range. As you are disappointedly thinking about leaving, an announcement comes over the intercom: "Attention shoppers: all our security systems are malfunctioning, so the mall will be closing now. Please leave the premises immediately."

- *What do you do?*
- *What do other shoppers do?*
- *Imagine you are a store owner, and "anything goes" for you as well. What do you do?*

Shift to the next activity by saying: *Laws and rules may sometimes put a crimp in your style, but the reality is, we need most of them to ensure society runs smoothly. We also need to accept the limits with which we have been created. This isn't always easy. Adam and Eve pushed their limits, and look what happened.*

3. EXPLORE THE BIBLE 8-10 minutes.

>> **Option A:** Stage a mock trial based on Genesis 3:1-19. Divide up the parts as follows: **Prosecutor**, **Judge** (God), The Defendants: **Adam**, **Eve**, the **Serpent**. The remainder of your group is the **jury**.

Spend 3-5 minutes reading over the passage and planning, then act it out. Go through courtroom procedure as closely as possible. Read the charge before each defendant, ask for a plea, let the jury give the verdict of guilty, and have God pass sentence using the material found in the passage. After the trial, ask Eve and the serpent how it felt to be blamed for the whole fiasco. Also ask:

- *How do you think Adam, Eve, and the serpent felt about their punishments?*
- *What happened to God's command to fill the earth with life? To till and keep the earth?*

>> **Facing a crisis of over-population...**

- Whenever we improve living conditions for people, the rate of their population growth decreases.

- Living populations are limited by lack of food, water, natural resources, space, and pollution. But through science and technology in medicine and agriculture, humans postpone nature's limitations.

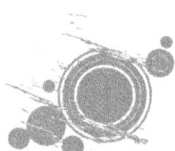

>>> **Option B:** Write the following questions where they can be seen by all. Ask participants to consider these questions as Genesis 3:1-19 is read aloud:

1. What convinced Eve to eat from the forbidden tree?
2. Why do you think Adam ate the fruit Eve gave him?
3. How did humanity's relationship with God change because of humanity's disobedience?
4. How did Adam and Eve's relationship change?
5. How have humanity's tasks of tilling, keeping, and filling the earth been affected?

Assign the parts of the serpent, Eve, Adam, God, and narrator. Read through the passage. Then discuss the questions briefly.

4. APPLY 10-20 minutes

Say: *There are limits to the world's resources, the abuse our environment can take, and our knowledge of how the world functions. Many environmental problems we face today are caused by failure to accept limits. When we refuse to recognize limits, the whole world suffers. But even with limits we can live well and make something beautiful. Let's put that idea into practice.*

>>> **Option A:** Hand out a pencil/pen, piece of paper, and a ruler or straightedge to each person. Give everyone 10 minutes to draw a basic floor plan of their "dream home."

Share the floor plans with each other, then discuss:

1. *How much living space does one person need?*
2. *The world has limited space. Would I be spending too much money on my personal comfort if I built my dream home? How much should I save to help others?*
3. *How does my plan fit with God's intention of abundance for all?*

"Creation provides a place for humans, but it is greater than humanity and within it even great [humans] are small…. We will have either to live within our limits, within the human definition, or not live at all."

Wendell Berry,
The Unsettling of America

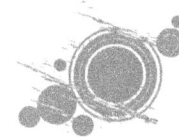

Our lifestyle choices demonstrate our care for God's earth and the human family. If we use up more than our share of the world's resources, we damage the environment as well as the ability of others to survive now and in the future, and tarnish what it means to be faithful to God.

Architects of sustainability: Now have everyone imagine that they've brought their plans to a group of *architects of sustainability*. Choose a few plans to focus on, and work together as architects to amend the plans to use as little space as possible, be energy efficient, cost effective, and still have features interesting enough to qualify as a dream home.

>>> **Option B:** Bring a box full of "garbage" into the center of the group. (Include: used paper, envelopes, egg cartons, glass jars, soda cans, old clothing, etc.) As a group, go through the box and think of how these items can be dealt with other than throwing them away. Keep in mind "God created a world out of chaos—what can I create out of this?"

>>> **Option C:** (for a camp/retreat/youth group setting):
As a group, make a quilt or rag-rug using only scrap material from old clothes. See what beautiful and useful things your group can produce within the limitations of old clothes! Ask a quilter or weaver in the congregation to help, and provide books with pictures of quilts or rugs to stimulate ideas.

As a **Respond** for this option, display your quilt/rug for your congregation. Include a statement explaining the limitations under which it was produced!

UNIT AFFIRMATION

We care for the earth because:

God made it;

God owns it;

God cares for it;

God wills it;

God speaks through it;

God acts in it.

Shantilal Bhagat, in "God's Earth Our Home."

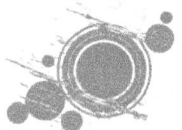

LOOK AHEAD

If you planned to use the Extender Session, do it next time you meet. You will need to invite an older person to the meeting to share about lifestyle changes, or do some research.

If you are going on to Session 5, record 3-4 minutes of commercials for the Apply option. If you are going to use the overnight campout option, start planning times and location now.

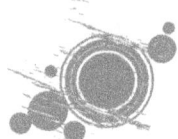

5. RESPOND 8-12 minutes

One way to take seriously our responsibility to care for the earth and live within limits is to make small changes to our lifestyle. There are many simple things an individual can do to use less energy and resources.

>> **Option A:** Encourage each person in your group to make a specific pledge to use fewer resources in the coming week—that is, impose consumption limits on themselves (e.g., walk/bike instead of driving, not buy junk food for ____ length of time, use reusable bags for shopping, use and wash glassware instead of disposable plates and cups). Make a poster listing your pledges. Hang the poster somewhere your parish will see it. Include an explanation that the youth are making these pledges as a step to living within the earth's limited resources.

Close by saying together the unit affirmation.

>> **Option B:** Yet another way to make a difference is to bring awareness of environmental issues to the attention of others. "Trash" the church sanctuary! Make sure to get permission, keep it a secret, use "clean" trash, and don't block the aisles. Also explain why you did it! An alternative could be to present a proposal for water collection, food gardening, or another use of church property.

After you make your plans, close by saying together the unit affirmation.

INSIGHTS FROM SCRIPTURE

Things couldn't be much better: A marvelous garden, ecologically balanced, providing people with food (Gen. 2:9) and meaningful work (Gen. 2:15). Possibilities abound, and there is only one limit, one tree from which fruit must not be eaten (Gen. 2:17). Things couldn't be much better. Or could they?

Humans seem never to have seen a limit they didn't try to breach. Intrigued by the "off-limits" God placed on the tree, humans take matters into their own hands and push the boundaries identified for them by God.

>> OVER THE LIMIT

Transgressing God's limits has dire consequences. First, there is a breakdown in humanity's relationship with God. Relying on their own judgment and overstepping their bounds with their creator meant the first people could no longer share the same closeness with God. Instead, they run to hide (Gen. 3:8).

Second, there is a breakdown in community. When God approaches the guilty pair, they begin pointing fingers, blaming each other for their disobedience. At the end of the line is the serpent, and no fingers with which to point. The community of mutual respect and trust is destroyed; it becomes a community of accusations.

Things get even worse in verses 16-19. God's sentencing was not so much a punishment as the recognition that ignoring God's limits alters human reality. Up until this point, man and woman existed in a situation of mutual love, respect, and responsibility. Now, the woman finds the man will rule over her (Gen. 3:16). By taking the mysteries of God into their own hands, humanity opens the way for inequality and oppression.

36 In Real Life | Keeping the Garden

Even the very blessings of humanity got tainted. There would be pain in childbirth (Gen. 1:28), and humanity's role as tiller and keeper of the earth would be characterized by hard work, sweat, and weeds (Gen. 3:17-19). God establishes limits on human behavior, and when we refuse to accept the limits of our creation, the whole world suffers, as well as our connection to the Creator.

>> A SUFFERING WORLD

Though nature is amazingly resilient and regenerative, there are limits to resources. The earth can only take so much air pollution, so much water contamination, so many parts per million of greenhouse gases before ecological balance is destroyed and natural processes malfunction.

Finally, there are limits to human knowledge. We do not understand all the effects of our actions. We cannot know all the results of how we have disrupted the natural processes of life. We try to bury our problems, such as garbage and radioactive waste, and hope they won't come back to haunt us.

But the tough question is, what *are* the limits? If God made people with minds able to dream up genetic engineering, medical advances, and increased production, how can we agree on what our limits are? Where is the balance between using our gifts to the fullest and moving past the point of diminishing returns? It will be an ongoing debate. But the irony is that just at the point in human history when we have the technology, communications, and wealth to end poverty and its stresses on the environment, we are also running out of time in which to do it.

When we ignore human limitations, we try to take the place of God. We trust ourselves. We begin to order life in ways that ignore God's calling, and are driven by our desires for convenience and comfort. We trust in the latest gadget, media-drenched popularity, and money to provide fulfillment. But it is never enough. We cannot relieve the anxiety in our lives and restore balance until we reunite with the harmony of God that is deep within life.

"If we are going to hold on to this place ...we will have to become the kind of people who can imagine a faraway, magical place like the Arctic National Wildlife Refuge—and all the oil beneath it—and declare that it is not ours to own because it already owns itself. It's going to demand the most selfless kind of love to do right by what we cherish, and give it the protection to flourish outside our possessive embrace."

Barbara Kingsolver,
Small Wonder

>>> **SESSION 5**

SUFFICIENCY >>>

Exploring tough questions facing youth today

>> KEY VERSES

[Cain said to God,] "Today you have driven me away from the soil, and I shall be hidden from your face; I shall be a fugitive and a wanderer on the earth, and anyone who meets me may kill me." Then the Lord said to him, "Not so! Whoever kills Cain will suffer a sevenfold vengeance." And the Lord put a mark on Cain, so that no one who came upon him would kill him. (Gen. 4:14-15)

>> FAITH STORY

Genesis 4:1-16

>> FAITH FOCUS

When Cain saw that God had rejected his offering but had accepted that of his brother Abel, he murdered Abel. We expect that Cain deserves to die. But instead God gave him what he needed, not what he deserved—grace. He was disciplined, but spared from death. God placed humanity in the world with what they needed to live full and healthy lives. When we try to take the abundance for ourselves, others are robbed of necessities and the whole world suffers.

>> SESSION GOAL

Challenge participants to look beyond themselves when evaluating their needs, wants, and dreams.

>> Materials needed and advance preparation

- Go over rules for the Focus activity, and have ready slips of paper, pens/pencils, place to write scoring table and team scores where everyone can see them.
- Writing paper
- Bibles
- Chalkboard/chalk or newsprint/marker
- 3-4 minutes of recorded commercials (clips) and viewing equipment; or video clips of *The Story of Stuff*; or collect magazines (see Apply *options*)
- Copies of both handout sheets for Session 5 (tailor questions to fit your group)
- Plan a time and location for an overnight trip (see Apply *Option D*).

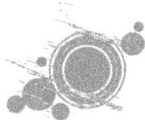

TEACHING PLAN

1. FOCUS 10-12 minutes

Divide into two teams. Explain that for this game each team will write either an X or a Y on a small slip of paper. Write the following scoring system where the groups can see it:

	Score			
	Team 1	Team 2	Team 1	Team 2
Choice:	X	Y	+5	-2
	Y	X	-2	+5
	X	X	-3	-3
	Y	Y	+2	+2

In Real Life | Keeping the Garden   **39**

The two teams must not talk to each other at any time during the game. If possible, teams should go to separate rooms or have one team stand outside the door for the duration of play.

For each round, collect a slip from each group, then inform them of the results. Do this by writing the choices on a large sheet of paper where everyone can see them, or by filling out one score sheet for each group. After a few rounds, the sheet should look something like this:

	Selection		Score		Total Score	
Round	Team 1	Team 2	Team 1	Team 2	Team 1	Team 2
1	X	Y	+5	-2	+5	-2
2	X	X	-3	-3	+2	-5
3	Y	X	-2	+5	0	0
4...						

Continue for at least 5 rounds.

2. CONNECT 3-5 minutes

Gather everyone together to talk about the game you just played:

- *How did you feel when the other team selected an X when you had picked a Y?*
- *Why did you select X? Why select Y's?*
- *What strategy seemed to work the best for BOTH teams?*

When we think only of ourselves, things often end up worse than ever. This game illustrates what happens when all we do is try to get ourselves ahead. Point out that if the teams had always picked Y's, after 5 rounds each team would have had 10 points, and the combined total score would have been +20. Compare that with your scores.

Shift to the next activity by saying: *The game we just played illustrates what happens when we try to grab as much as we can for ourselves without considering others. Everyone suffers. A guy named Cain learned the hard way that God provides what we need, not what we think we deserve.*

3. EXPLORE THE BIBLE 10-15 minutes

Divide into two groups. Assign each group one of the perspectives listed on the handout sheet. Instruct each group to read the Bible passage with the corresponding questions in mind.

Give each group several minutes to write a letter from their assigned perspectives. Read the letters to each other once they have been completed.

4. APPLY 10-15 minutes

Like for Cain, God provides what we need, not what we deserve. God placed humanity in the world with what they needed to live full and healthy lives. But if some grab the abundance, others are robbed of bare necessities and the whole world suffers.

>>> **Option A:** Ask participants to consider the following questions (write them on the chalkboard or newsprint) as they watch 3-4 minutes of commercials. Discuss the observations. (**Alternative:** Instead of a clip, give each person a magazine full of ads to flip through. Discuss the same questions.)

1. *How many of the things advertised are needed for basic survival?*
2. *Do the advertisers connect buying their product with the fact that North Americans use far more than their share of the earth's resources? Do they want us to weigh our purchases against the fact that millions of people do not have enough to eat?*
3. *Do the advertisers make connections between their products and how their production and use hurts the environment?*

>>> **Option B:** View one or more short videos in Annie Leonard's *The Story of Stuff*, particularly The Story of Stuff and The Story of Solutions. (Some are found on YouTube.) Use some of the questions listed in *Option C* to debrief the viewing (http://storyofstuff.org/).

>>> **Option C:** Make a list of everything you would pack to camp for one week in an area where there are no stores or garbage cans. Once the list is complete, cut it in half. Keep only those things necessary for survival for one week.

Say, *We have much more than we actually need to survive. Most of us in North America could give away more than half of our possessions and still live more "comfortably" than most people in other countries.*

Discuss the following questions:

1. *Do we deserve to have so much while so many others have so little? Why or why not?*
2. *How do your "extra things" harm the environment?* (Use more than my share of energy; manufacturing unnecessary goods causes pollution; so busy accumulating extras I don't have time to reuse, make gifts, or bike where I need to go)

>>> **Option D:** (for a camp/retreat setting):

Plan to go on a camping trip as described in *Option C* above, but only overnight. As a group, list everything you'll need, then decide together how to whittle half the items from the list. Throughout this process keep in mind the question, "What do we really need to survive?"

Note: Be sure the trip is well-supervised and conducted in a safe manner. Guide the group to wise decisions, and camp close to shelter should it be needed. The idea is to see what you can do without, not give everyone the worst night of their lives.

5. RESPOND 10-12 minutes

It's easy to say that we live in a society that uses too much of the world's resources. It's much harder to look at ourselves and see places where we can cut down. If we are to care faithfully for and honor God's creation, we need to reassess what is sufficient, and share abundance.

Some people in the group may point out that what we leave may just mean more for others who already have plenty. Point out that it may be so, but that we are responsible for our own lifestyle choices and our own relationship with God. If our example eventually catches on, great. Even if it doesn't, we'll have maintained our integrity with God and creation.

UNIT AFFIRMATION

We care for the earth because:

God made it;

God owns it;

God cares for it;

God wills it;

God speaks through it;

God acts in it.

Shantilal Bhagat, in "God's Earth Our Home."

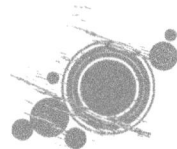

>>> **Option A:** (This option could follow nicely if you used the "trash the church" option in Session 4.) Conduct a "Sustainability Audit" of your church building (see handout sheet). Identify areas where your congregation could cut down on its use of resources. Use the list on the handout sheet to determine your church's Sustainability Score. (If some questions are not suitable for your church, or the answers are unavailable, substitute a different environmental consideration in the lines provided.)

Brainstorm how your group could work to reduce your church's use of resources (e.g., carpool to church functions, don't use disposables at meals or snacks, buy only recycled products, etc.).

Think of ways that your church could go beyond the suggestions in this list. How could your church get closer to a score of 100 and still function in North American society?

>>> **Option B:** This option helps participants think about how they can use less so that others have more. Have each person think of three things they have but aren't using (clothes, books, electronics, games, etc.). Make a list of these things on a chalkboard or newsprint.

Make a second list of people or organizations who could benefit from the types of things you have listed (thrift stores, shelters, etc.). Ask: *Are you willing to give these things up?* If the group is willing, arrange a time and day to collect the items. Donate them to the organizations or people who can use them.

Close with the unit affirmation printed on page 30 (or on handout sheet).

LOOK AHEAD

Arrange for a member of your congregation to play the part of "Noah" in Session 6. Collect tissue boxes for building an altar (see Apply.) If you plan to use the tree-planting option for Respond, find a sapling to plant.

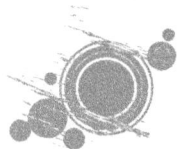

INSIGHTS FROM SCRIPTURE

Although this passage is often called the story of "Cain and Abel," Abel is a minor character in this drama. He's a name, a body, whose main act in the story is to die. The narrative is most concerned with the interaction between Cain and God.

This story gives no reason why God rejected Cain's sacrifice and accepted that of his younger brother. Instead, it asks, "What will Cain do about it?" Will he master the sin that is waiting for him just around the corner (Gen. 4:7)? How will Cain react to a turn of events that appears arbitrary and unfair?

Cain blows it. He figures if he couldn't have God's blessing, then neither should his brother.

LIVING WITH THE CONSEQUENCES

Once Abel is dead, the primary question shifts to God: What are the consequences for this horrible crime? How will God respond?

The results are devastating. The violation of his brother affects Cain's entire being. His relationship with others is severed; he is separated from community, and forced to live as a wanderer (Gen. 4:12). His relationship with the environment is also affected; the land that provided in the past becomes the source of a curse (Gen. 4:11-12). Finally, the relationship between Cain and God suffers; Cain would be hidden from the face of the divine (Gen. 4:14), and would no longer live in God's presence (Gen. 4:16).

TO LIVE A GOD-CENTERED LIFE

Our lives are filled with situations beyond our control that seem arbitrary and unfair. We see what others have, and want it for ourselves. God challenges us to respond to these situations in a positive way, and not to allow the sin lurking at the door to rule our hearts.

God calls us to keep our lives centered on God alone. When we let self-centeredness rule our actions, we violate those around us. We sever our relationship with others; we value the things we possess more than the world around us. We grab the earth's plenty for ourselves, robbing others of the necessities of life and at the same time jeopardizing future generations. We also affect our relationship with the environment. When Cain's relationship with God crashed, so did his connection to the land (Gen. 4:12). That is what makes our relationship with the environment so unmistakably a faith issue.

GOD'S GIFT OF GRACE

Don't miss the surprise at the end of this murder drama. When Cain complained that someone might kill him in his wanderings, we might assume he was only getting what he deserved, and none too soon. We expect God to say some divine equivalent to "tough beans!" Instead, God protected Cain. Despite the terrible evil that Cain had done, God was interested in restoration, giving Cain the grace he needed, not the punishment he deserved.

God placed humanity in the world with what they needed to live full and healthy lives. But the excesses of the developed world are wreaking ecological, economic, and social havoc on the whole planet. We must master the sin that is lurking at our door, lest we kill our brothers and sisters, severing our relationship with the rest of the world and with God.

"The idea of infite or unlimited growth, which proves so attractive to economists, financiers and experts in technology… is based on the lie that there is an infinite supply of the earth's goods, and this leads to the planet being squeezed dry at every limit."

Pope Francis, *On Care for Our Common Home*, 106.

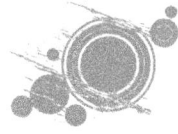

Write a Letter

Exploring tough questions facing youth today

Group 1
Write a letter to God from Cain's perspective. Consider the following:

- What thoughts and impulses crowded your mind when God turned down your offering, but accepted Abel's?

- Does God's punishment fit your crime?

- How can you live with the consequences of your action?

- Why would God grant you mercy by protecting your life?

Group 2
Write a letter to Cain from God's perspective. Consider the following:

- Why would you turn down Cain's offering, but accept Abel's?

- How did you feel when you were punishing Cain?

- Why did you offer Cain the mercy of protecting his life?

Permission is granted to photocopy this handout for use with this session.

SUSTAINABILITY AUDIT

for _____
(name of your parish)

Church bulletin printed on recycled paper?	+5
No bulletin used?	+10
Scrap office paper reused (e.g., for memo paper)?	+10
Used paper sorted and recycled? Newspapers	+5
All paper	+10
System for recycling aluminum and glass?	+10
System in place for recycling plastics?	+10
Disposable dishes used . . . Never?	+10
For coffee/snack?	0
For potlucks?	-10
All lighting is energy-efficient LED?	+10
CFLs?	+5
Church heat/air conditioning turned down when building not in use?	+10
Water efficient toilets or toilet dams used (e.g., brick in the tank)?	+10
Church members carpool to church functions . . . Most of the time?	+10
Sometimes?	+5
Never?	0
Church is a part of a North American society that consumes far more than its share of the earth's resources?	-50

_____
_____
_____
_____

Total_____

Keeping the Garden : Session 5

Permission is granted to photocopy this handout for use with this session.

>>> **SESSION 6**

FAITH IN THE RAIN >>>

>> KEY VERSES

The Lord saw that the wickedness of humankind was great in the earth, and that every inclination of the thoughts of their hearts was only evil continually. But Noah found favor in the sight of the Lord. (Gen. 6:5, 8)

>> FAITH STORY

Genesis 6:5–9:17

>> FAITH FOCUS

Noah lived in a time when the world was disintegrating. Things were so bad that God decided to flood the world. But Noah lived a righteous life and followed the direction God gave him. Through him, God restored the earth and made it rich and fertile once again. When we respond faithfully to God's calling, God works through us to bring about the restoration of the earth.

>> SESSION GOAL

Reassure participants that God uses small acts of faith to accomplish great healing in humanity's relationship with creation.

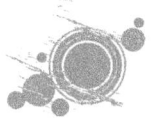

TEACHING PLAN

1. FOCUS 3-5 minutes

Start people thinking about how valuable one person can be. Give everyone in your group at least one piece of the puzzle you have prepared, but keep one hidden for yourself. Allow participants a few moments to put the puzzle together using their pieces.

At the end, you should have the complete picture, minus the one piece. Ask the participants what they think of the result; how does it look? Is it complete? Comment on how one small piece can affect the look of an entire puzzle.

Produce the missing piece and complete the picture.

>> Materials needed and advance preparation

- Find or make a simple puzzle for your group to put together, one with enough pieces for each person (including yourself) to have one.
- Pens and pencils
- Copies of the handout sheet for Session 6
- Invite an older person from your congregation to portray Noah, complete with rain slicker and boots, hat, etc. Noah should prepare by using the Bible passage, insights from Scripture, and the suggested answers to the questions (see Explore the Bible).
- Prepare blocks with earthkeeping principles written in large letters (facial tissue boxes would work well) (see Apply).
- Song books; arrange for piano or guitar accompaniment if possible (see Respond Option A).
- Obtain a small tree and shovel, and locate a suitable place for planting (see Respond Option C)

In Real Life | Keeping the Garden   47

2. CONNECT 7-9 minutes

Distribute copies of the handout sheet for Session 6, and a pen or pencil to each person. Allow time to jot down endings to the sentences under Real Value.

1. I feel powerless at home when...
2. I feel important at home when...
3. I feel powerless at school when...
4. I feel important at school when...
5. I feel powerless about environmental issues when...
6. I feel important about environmental issues when...

»» Option A: Collect the papers. Read through the various responses to the statements, taking care to keep responses anonymous.

»» Option B: Instead of collecting the papers, discuss your answers as a group. Involve as many people as possible in sharing their thoughts on each question.

Shift to the next activity by saying: *When we look at tackling environmental problems, it seems that we are up against an insurmountable task. But when we respond faithfully to God's love for creation, even one person can work toward the restoration of God's plans for the world.*

»»
REDUCE,
REUSE,
RECYCLE

Many can recite the mantra, "Reduce, Reuse, Recycle." But ever wonder why recycling is #3? It's not because it fits there poetically. Recycling, while good, is the least efficient treatment of resources. It fools us into thinking we can consume huge quantities of resources without guilt. First, reduce!

3. EXPLORE THE BIBLE 15-20 minutes

Read aloud Genesis 6:11-22. As you read, have Noah enter. You might even interrupt yourself to welcome Noah, the resident expert on the story of the flood. Ask him to sit in your circle while you conduct an interview using some of the following questions. Noah should embellish the answers, using the suggested responses and information from **Insights from Scripture**.

1. *What was the world like back before the flood?*
Responses:
   - No movies, cars, or airplanes
   - People had stopped caring about anyone but themselves
   - Not easy to be a follower of God

2. *What did you think when God first asked you to build an ark?*
   - First reaction, "Yeah, right!" Didn't believe it.
   - Felt unworthy—why should God single me out like that?
   - Confused, scared—didn't know what was going to happen.
   - Wasn't sure that God wouldn't suddenly change plans and do away with everything—even the ark! God was really irked!

3. *Did you know beforehand how many days it would rain?*
   - Wasn't sure what was going to happen.
   - God didn't fill in all the details.

4. *How did you feel when you were drifting on the high seas?*
   - Sad for the entire world. It had become really messed up, but it was the only world I knew.
   - Some doubts—wasn't sure if God might suddenly change plans even then.
   - Wasn't sure that God would stop the rain and let the waters subside.

5. *What was it like to be locked up for forty days and forty nights with all those animals?*
   - Just imagine!

6. *What was the first thing you did once the waters had subsided and you could get out of the ark?*
   - Jumped out and kissed the ground.
   - Built an altar and made an offering to God for preserving us through the flood.

7. *What were your feelings when you saw the rainbow?*
   - Relieved—God was there for us.
   - Thankful that God would not destroy the world again.
   - The most beautiful sight ever seen, and the greatest promise made to anyone was made to all of us.

Add your own questions. Provide an opportunity for people to ask Noah questions. End the interview with:

8. *What advice would you give to us today?*
   - Listen to God, even when it isn't the easy way out.
   - If you are open, God will use you to restore the world, to help ensure it fulfills God's intention for it.
   - Have hope. God is faithful. We just need to be faithful to God.
   - Practice gratitude. God's grace allows us to live. Be sure to thank God for the life we are given.

Thank Noah for taking the time to visit.

> "Yet all is not lost. Human beings, while capable of the worst, are also capable of rising above themselves, choosing again what is good, and making a new start."

Pope Francis, *On Care for Our Common Home*, 205.

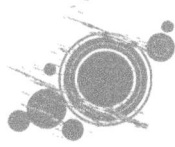

4. APPLY 8-10 minutes

[**Note:** If you didn't present Annie Leonard's *The Story of Stuff* (http://storyofstuff.org/), show it here.]

Many environmental problems are the result of millions of people doing little things. One person driving to work isn't much of a problem. It's a different story when we're talking about millions of people driving to work every day. Small acts have caused many environmental problems. It will be small acts that will make a difference in the long run.

Prior to meeting, prepare blocks (using facial tissue boxes or the like) with the following principles written in large letters (substitute or add other appropriate ones as you see fit):

One by one, show participants the blocks you have prepared:

Live simply	Recognize limits
Practice gratitude	Keep the earth
Protect life	Preserve biodiversity
Listen to the past	Name appropriately
Share resources	Serve creation

Consider each principle in turn. As you hold a block, brainstorm for practical ways the principle can be lived out. Once you have finished discussing each block, hand it to someone. Use the blocks to build an altar, like Noah did, in the middle of the circle.

5. RESPOND 7-15 minutes

Encourage people to consider one concrete change they could make in their lives to be more faithful in caring for God's creation. (These could be some of the same commitments they've made in other sessions.) Write or draw goals on the handout sheet under Playing for Change.

Once everyone has written down a goal, announce that we cannot achieve a proper relationship with the environment on our own. We need the Creator's help. Invite participants to come to the altar you built and place their slips of paper as a symbolic offering to God. By placing this offering, we are asking God to shape us into a new creation, one that fulfills the creative intentions in our relationship with the environment.

>> **Option A:** Close by singing "Tend the Ground" by Curtis Stephan (inspired by Pope Francis' encyclical), "All the Ends of the Earth" by Bob Dufford, S.J., "Send Us Your Spirit" by David Haas, or a similar song of your choosing. You could also watch the following music video of So Will I (100 Billion X) (https://www.youtube.com/watch?v=W7Vql7WhZ_U). After the song, speak the Unit Affirmation together.

>> **Option B:** Close with prayer. Begin by asking God to make each of you a new creation, one fulfilling God's intended relationship between humanity and creation. Allow each member of the group to add a prayer of their own. Do not force anyone to pray out loud.

Conclude the prayer with an appeal for help to live a life faithful to God, then close with the unit affirmation.

>> **Option C:** Plant a tree on your church or camp yard as a symbol of hope and your group's commitment to living in proper relationship with God's creation. Close with the unit affirmation.

UNIT AFFIRMATION

We care for the earth because:

God made it;

God owns it;

God cares for it;

God wills it;

God speaks through it;

God acts in it.

Shantilal Bhagat, in "God's Earth Our Home."

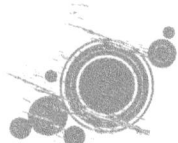

INSIGHTS FROM SCRIPTURE

Although God affirmed the world as being very good (Gen. 1:31), creation is out of step with the creator. Adam and Eve refused to accept the limits of their creation. Cain murdered Abel and was alienated from God. By the time of Noah, God concluded that humanity completely ignored the good purposes for which people were created. People were so out of touch with creation's original intent, God was sorry ever to have created the world.

Just when things seemed darkest, however, a glimmer of hope appeared in the person of Noah. Even as the rains began to fall, and in deepest sorrow at the unfaithfulness of creation, God set out, through Noah, to restore creation.

Noah responded to God's leading in faith. This is not because following God was the easy way out. Looking utterly foolish to others, Noah constructed the ark to God's exact specifications, filled it with the right number of animals, and trusted in God's protection.

Chapter 8:1 represents the turning point. Because Noah was faithful, God restored the earth and made it rich and fertile. Because the "inclination of the human heart is evil from youth" (Gen. 8:21), God gave nature a new status more independent from humans, so that the agricultural seasons would be ensured against human immorality (Gen. 8:21-22).

This new approach came about because God still desired a world full of life, where people live in proper relationship with the environment, with each other, and with God. But we sometimes get disheartened. Self-centered humanity, the refusal to keep within God's limits, and our failure to fulfill the role of stewards/servants of creation all threaten our very survival. We see chaos returning in the destruction of forests and ecosystems, the poisoning of lakes and rivers, and the fouling of the atmosphere.

However, God uses faithful people to respond to the challenges facing creation. God calls us to radical action, to be faithful to God's commands and guidance. When we give our lives over to God, we can be a vehicle for the restoration of a hurting world. By responding to God with faith, we receive the peace that comes with aligning ourselves with the intent of the Creator.

Real Value

Exploring tough questions facing youth today

1. I feel powerless at home when...
   _____

2. I feel important at home when...
   _____

3. I feel powerless at school when...
   _____

4. I feel important at school when...
   _____

5. I feel powerless about environmental issues when...
   _____

6. I feel important about environmental issues when...
   _____

"Yet all is not lost. Human beings, while capable of the worst, are also capable of rising above themselves, choosing again what is good, and making a new start."

Pope Francis, *On Care for Our Common Home*, 205.

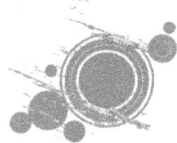

Playing for Change

One concrete change I can make to more faithfully care for God's creation. (Could be one of the same commitments you made in another session.) Write or draw your commitment here.

Keeping the Garden : Session 6

Many can recite the mantra, "Reduce, Reuse, Recycle." But ever wonder why recycling is #3? It's not because it fits there poetically. Recycling, while good, is the least efficient treatment of resources. It fools us into thinking we can consume huge quantities of resources without guilt. First, reduce!

Permission is granted to photocopy this handout for use with this session.

>>> EXTENDER SESSION

ONCE UPON A TIME...

>> Option A: . . . we lived this way.

>> SESSION GOAL

Help participants draw on sustainable practices from the past in developing their own caring relationship with God's creation.

>> SESSION PLAN

People have short memories. We forget what the world used to be like. We forget which areas used to be forest, which streams used to have fish, and how clean the air used to be.

We also forget that society didn't always use so many resources. Many of our parents and grandparents grew up with a much simpler lifestyle. Learning from older generations can help us develop a more faithful relationship with God's creation.

Invite an older person from your congregation to speak with your group. Ask someone who has lived in your area for most of their life, and has experienced many of the changes society has experienced over the last 50 years.

Alternatively, do some research on your local area in a community library, museum, or online.

Ask questions in the following areas:

1. The natural environment. How has the local environment changed?
   - state of streams and lakes?
   - amount of air pollution?
   - amount of forests?
   - reduction of numbers and types of wild animals?
   - amount of land left "untouched" by humans?
   - number of houses, freeways, and buildings in area?

2. Ways of doing things. How has life changed?
   - amount of resources/energy used?
   - number of electronic gadgets found in kitchens?
   - movement from reusing/recycling to disposables?
   - amount of driving people do?
   - expectations of standard of living?

> >>>
> "Aren't there things that just have to be thrown away?" I ask.
> "There's no such place as 'away,'" he replies.
> "So all of those wastes from the farm, the home, the lumberyard, and the fishing boats shouldn't be going to the landfill?"
> "It's not waste," says Gregory. "It's not waste until it's wasted."
>
> William Bryant Logan, *Dirt: The Ecstatic Skin of the Earth*

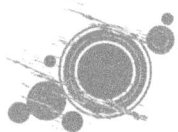

3. How do you think the world needs to change if we are to better connect with God's creation?

Add questions, and invite participants to ask their own. Conclude by discussing ways we can use knowledge of the past to help the environment today.

›› Option B: . . . this soil was compost.
(for camp or retreat setting)

›› SESSION GOAL

Teach participants how to compost, a specific skill for "keeping the garden."

›› SESSION PLAN

Engage the help of a gardener in your congregation who composts regularly. Set a time and place for getting together to add organic material to a compost pile, help turn a pile, or make new plantings in soil derived from compost. Have the gardener explain the concepts of composting, and, if possible, have participants smell some "finished" compost—newly made soil ready for using again. Contrast this with the smell of the new "waste" just added.

Demonstrate ways participants can start a compost pile either at home, or even at church (using grass clippings, kitchen waste from church meals, etc.). Perhaps some youth will even volunteer to oversee the composting project for the church.

Most of all, point out how this "making of soil" is a small, concrete step in:

- demonstrating faithful care for the earth
- being willing to learn more about this substance foundational to the world God created
- how large-scale composting can be an alternative to creating more landfills
- a visible way to reuse resources.

Exploring tough questions facing youth today

CLUELESS AND CALLED
Discipleship and the Gospel of Mark

What does it take to be a disciple? This study of the Gospel of Mark focuses on the requirements for following Jesus' way and the abundant life that is ours as a result. (5 sessions)

DO MIRACLES HAPPEN?
Signs and Wonders in the Gospel of John

The greatest miracle, recorded in John 1:14 and 3:16, is the miracle of God's love that became flesh and lived among us. But John also included examples of what we more traditionally think of as miracles: the wonder of abundance from little; healing; signs of impossibility and faith; and the resurrection. (5 sessions)

DO THE RIGHT THING
Ethics Shaped by Faith

How do you know what's right and what's wrong? Even when you figure it out, the right thing is often the unpopular or unpleasant choice. This unit offers participants a clearer sense of what it means to claim a faith identity, a foundation that can help them sort out the gritty details of ethics shaped by faith. (6 sessions)

FIGHT RIGHT
A Christian Approach to Conflict Resolution

This unit will help youth understand conflict and its function. They will learn how they can be honest and loving, and explore how conflict can be used for positive results. They will also learn ways to enhance their communication skills. 1 Corinthians. (5 sessions)

GOD IS A WARRIOR?
Violence in the Bible

The Bible challenges us to be reconciled to one another and work for justice. So what do we do with the stories that seem to condone violence or even encourage it? A discussion of issues in the Old and New Testaments. (6 sessions)

HOW DO YOU KNOW?
Wisdom in the Bible

Wisdom literature teaches us that we gain knowledge of the world, ourselves, and God through experience and observation. This unit provides practical, hands-on wisdom to help young people avoid life's snares and grow closer to God. Proverbs, Job, Ecclesiastes. (5 sessions)

HOW TO BE A TRUE FRIEND
The Bible Reveals Friendship's Heart

To be a friend takes skill. Help youth discover the secrets of friendship through various stories from the Old and New Testament. (6 sessions)

HOW TO READ THE BIBLE
Building Skills for Bible Study

What kind of book is the Bible? What does this book mean to me? This unit looks at the Bible as revelation, as history, as literature. Selected scripture. (5 sessions)

KEEPING THE GARDEN
A Faith Response to God's Creation

If Christians believe that God made the world, we do not need any more compelling reason to care for it than that God has handed us a treasure to hold and protect. This unit gets beyond trendy environmentalism and challenges youth to see environmental awareness as a religious issue. Genesis. (6 sessions)

MANTRAS, MENORAHS, AND MINARETS
Encountering Other Faiths

How is Christianity different from other faiths? Why do others believe the way they do? This study can give youth a new appreciation for the uniqueness of Jesus. Selected scripture. (5 sessions)

SALT, LIGHT, AND THE GOOD LIFE
The Beatitudes and the Sermon on the Mount

What can youth expect in a life of discipleship? This unit explores the Sermon on the Mount under four main sections: the Beatitudes, Salt and Light, Jesus and the Law, and Heavenly Teachings. Matthew 5. (6 sessions)

A SPECK IN THE UNIVERSE
The Bible on Self-Esteem and Peer Pressure

Discover God's unconditional love and acceptance of all people. This study will show positive ways to have one's life make a difference, and help youth find ways to resist negative peer pressure and turn it into positive action. (6 sessions)

THE RADICAL REIGN
Parables of Jesus

Jesus used parables to reveal what the kingdom of God is like, and how God relates to us. This study highlights how the parables reveal God's reign as radically different from the world we live in, and what that means for the Christian life. (6 sessions)

TESTING THE WATERS
Basic Tenets of Faith

Discover the biblical roots for the central Christian concepts of covenant, community, and baptism. This short course is a way to test the (baptismal) waters of Christianity before diving in, or review the basics for those who already have. (6 sessions)

WHO IS GOD?
Engaging the Mystery

God is beyond human comprehension, yet desires to be known. These sessions focus on the way we get clues about and glimpses of God from the Bible, God's creation, and church tradition. Selected scripture. (5 sessions)

www.ingramcontent.com/pod-product-compliance
Lightning Source LLC
Chambersburg PA
CBHW080408170426
43193CB00016B/2850